Down By The Praise Pond

Written by
Sherry Ludwig Kepley

Illustrated by
Lisa Albinus

Down By The Praise Pond

Published by Encouragement Cafe' Press
PO Box 1237
Clemmons, NC 27012

Scripture taken from the New King James Version®. Copyright © 1982 by Thomas Nelson. Used by permission. All rights reserved.

Scripture quotations marked HCSB are taken from the Holman Christian Standard Bible®, used by Permission HCSB ©1999, 2000, 2002, 2003, 2009 Holman Bible Publishers.

Holman Christian Standard Bible®, Holman CSB®, and HCSB® are federally registered trademarks of Holman Bible Publishers.

Scriptures taken from the Holy Bible, New International Version®, NIV®. Copyright © 1973, 1978, 1984, 2011 by Biblica, Inc.™ Used by permission of Zondervan. All rights reserved worldwide. www.zondervan.com The "NIV" and "New International Version" are trademarks registered in the United States Patent and Trademark Office by Biblica, Inc.®

All rights reserved.
No part of this book may be reproduced or used in any form, without written permission from the publisher.
©2021

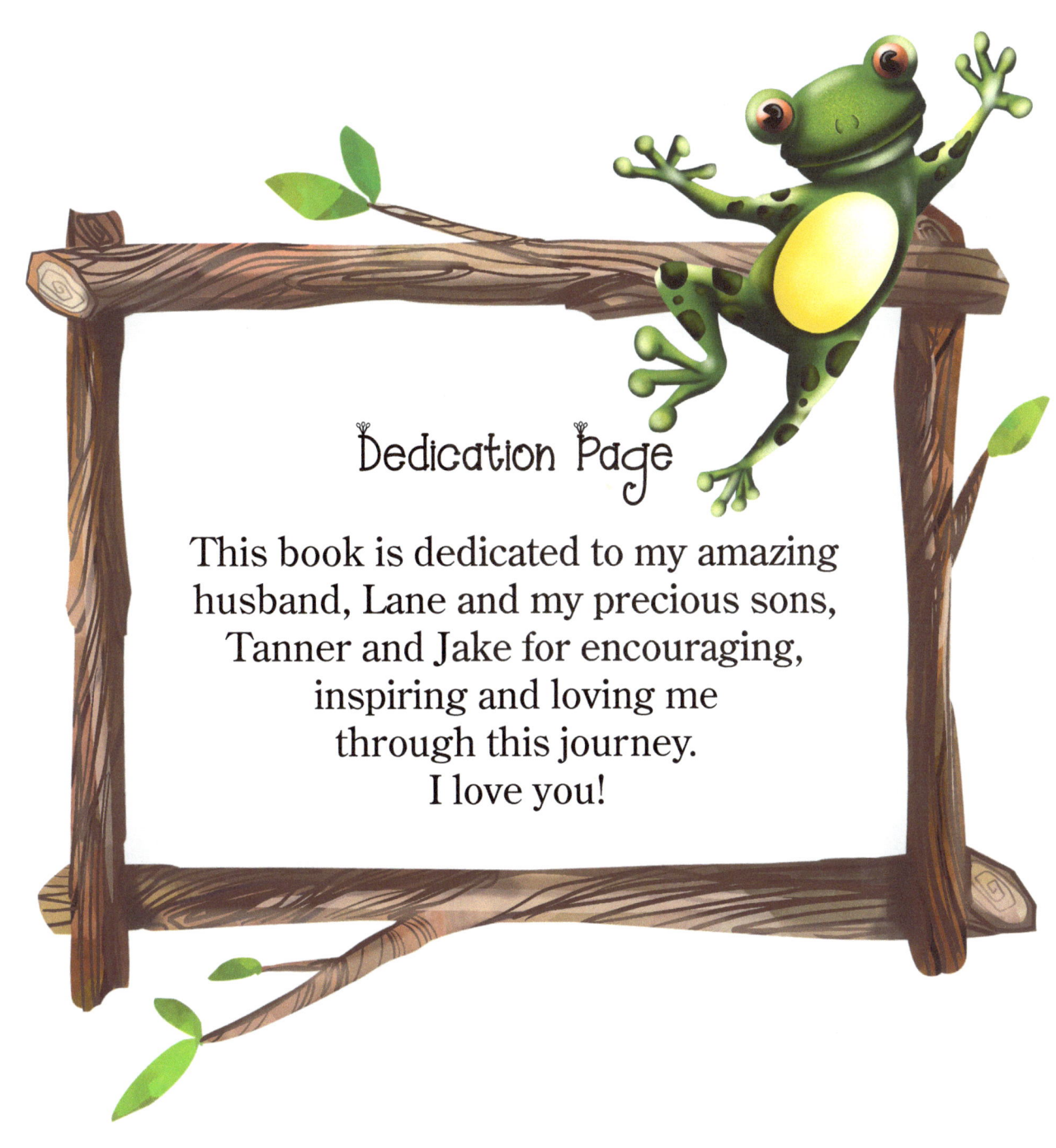

Dedication Page

This book is dedicated to my amazing husband, Lane and my precious sons, Tanner and Jake for encouraging, inspiring and loving me through this journey.
I love you!

Table of Contents

Phoebe The Firefly 7

Ace The Crane 15

Lucybelle The Butterfly 23

Ranger The Duck 31

Webster The Otter 39

Larue The Turtle 47

T. J. The Bullfrog 55

Sunday At The Praise Pond 63

Phoebe The Firefly

Phoebe the firefly stirred when the sun began to shine.
The bluebirds sang a melody from high up in the pine.
Phoebe spread her tiny wings as the breeze began to blow.
Excited by what the day would bring, she was ready to go.
The sky was blue. The clouds were white.
The air was warm and sweet.
She saw the pond just up ahead.
Her time with God was a treat.

Phoebe floated above the pond with its lily pads of green.
Dancing sunlight on the water was such a pretty scene.
The Praise Pond was so full of life with creatures all around.

She sang her praises to the Lord.
Oh, what a joyful sound!
But even as Phoebe sang, she had something to confess.
A secret she had hidden weighed heavily on her chest.

Phoebe didn't like the dark. She had been too afraid to tell.
After all, she's a firefly with a light upon her tail.
She brought her worries and her cares and shared with God each one.
He showed her that she's never alone since she had trusted in His Son.
God had given Phoebe the faith to fight her fears.
Jesus watches over her, and He is always near.

She didn't need to be afraid when the evening sky grew dim.
Every minute of the day she put her trust in Him
Now Phoebe shines the light of Jesus for everyone to see.
The love that Jesus has for her, He has for you and me.
So always come to Jesus with what is weighing on your mind.
He is the very best friend that you will ever find.

Your word is a lamp to my feet
and a light to my path.
Psalm 119:105 (NKJV)

Ace The Crane

Standing in the golden grass was a handsome whooping crane.
His legs were long, his wings were strong, and Ace was his name.
Staring into the Praise Pond, he was on a mission to catch some food.
Ace was doing some fishing and was careful not to move.

Not having very much luck, he had to come up with a new plan.
Ace really needed a bird's eye view,
and he couldn't get that on land.
But there was one big problem. What was Ace going to do?
He had to conquer his fear of heights to fly in the sky of blue.
Flying had always been Ace's dream,
since he was a small baby bird.
The only way to conquer his fear
was to put his trust in God's Word.

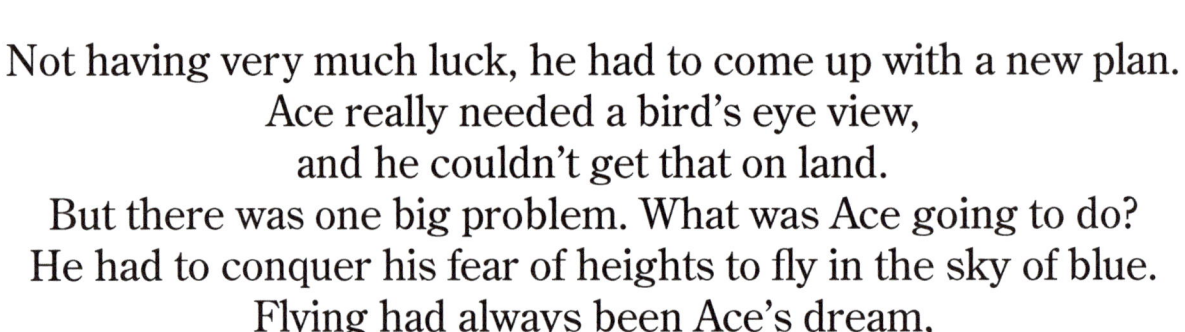

We are supposed to be strong and courageous
and should not be afraid.
Jesus is with us wherever we go, just like the Bible has said.
Ace talked to God at the Praise Pond.
He always found comfort there.

After giving all of his worries to God,
it was time to get in the air!
Although his legs were trembling,
he stretched his wings out wide.
Ace looked up at the bright blue sky,
knowing Jesus was right by his side.
Feeling his body lift off of the ground, his worries faded away.
God gave Ace the courage he needed
to make his dreams come true that day.

The Praise Pond looked so different from in the sky above.
God's creation was beautiful. A perfect display of His love.
So the next time you find yourself worried
and you've held it in for too long;
Remember that the Bible says, when we're weak,
our God is strong.

Be strong and courageous,
all you who put your hope in the Lord.
Psalm 31:24 (HCSB)

Lucybelle The Butterfly

It was such a beautiful morning.
The grass sparkled with the dew.
The sunshine peeked up over the trees.
The day was fresh and new.
A sweet fragrance filled the air from the honeysuckle vines.
The Praise Pond felt so peaceful surrounded by the pines.

The sunlight shining on her wings. Lucybelle was a lovely sight.
Dressed in stunning colors of purple, black, and white.
She was a beautiful butterfly, dancing on a gentle breeze.
She fluttered her wings for all to see, including the honeybees.
Lucybelle was full of pride, and she put on a show that day.
The honeybees didn't like it much, and they quickly flew away.
"Why don't the honeybees like me?" She just couldn't understand.
"I was sure they would be impressed. My wings are perfectly grand."

Floating down to the Praise Pond, she decided to sit for a spell.
She did a lot of thinking about why things didn't go so well.
Then Lucybelle folded her butterfly wings
and bowed her head to pray.
"Dear God, please forgive me for the way I acted today.
I'm sorry for not being humble and for being so full of pride."

Then God showed her that true beauty comes from
who you are on the inside.
Sitting by the Praise Pond, her heart was happy and light.
Lucybelle flew to the honeybee hive.
She needed to make things right.

She told them she was sorry and that God helped her understand.
We're each a masterpiece to Him, created by His own hand.
So never think you're more special than anyone else you see.
God made each of us exactly the way He wanted us to be.

Be clothed with humility, for "God resists the proud, but gives grace to the humble."
1Peter 5:5 (NKJV)

Ranger The Duck

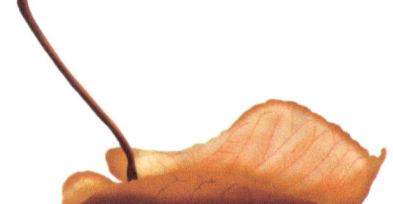

The seasons had changed,
and summer had come to an end.
Now the trees appeared to glow,
swaying in the brisk autumn wind.
The water reflected the changing leaves,
fiery orange, yellow and red.
Swimming across the pond was a mallard duck
with green feathers on his head.

Ranger was always patrolling the pond but never seemed to smile.
He was known as a grumpy duck,
and he had been that way for a while.
Years ago, as a duckling, something tragic happened to Ranger.
Although he was kind at heart, he had held on to his anger.
Someone he loved had to go away,
and he carried the hurt deep inside.
Ranger couldn't let go of the pain, no matter how hard he tried.

Then one day it became too much to carry the weight of it all.
Ranger cried out, "Please help me," and God heard his call.

The love of God poured over him and healed his heart that day.
The walls that he had built around himself
crumbled and fell away.
God took away Ranger's anger, and joy took its place.
He was thankful for the Praise Pond and God's amazing grace.

Now Ranger quacks to one and all as he patrols the pond each day.
Looking after his neighbors as he goes along his way.
God is always there for us and wants our trust in Him to grow.
He can heal a broken heart, and then His love in us will show.

He heals the brokenhearted
and binds up their wounds.
Psalm 147:3 (NKJV)

Webster The Otter

Stars like diamonds draped the midnight sky,
and the oaks were completely bare.
The leaves had long since blown away
in the rush of the blustery air.
Moonlight poured down from the sky onto the dark water below.
The Praise Pond looked just like a gift wrapped up
in the glistening snow.

Hunkered down at the edge of the pond
was the most hilarious sight.
A passel of otters with coats of fur were playing in the moonlight.
Sliding over mounds of snow, they made such a happy sound.
Until one of them began to push the others around.
Webster was the bossy one and picked what games to play.
If his friends didn't play along, Webster would pout all day.
But he had been bossy too many times,
and his otter friends were through.
It was their turn to pick a game,
and they wanted to play something new.

The otters swam across the pond, but Webster didn't go.
He watched them have a snowball fight, and they built a fort in the snow.
As Webster stood there all alone, God brought something to his mind.
He wasn't being a very good friend, and he hadn't been very kind.

The Bible says, "Do to others as you would have them do to you." That is what Jesus taught in His word, and that is what we should do.

Webster could see that he had not behaved that way with his friends.
He swam to them as fast as he could. He wanted to make amends.
His friends were so excited when Webster came back to play.
If you want to be a good friend, Jesus can show you the way.

Do to others as you would have them do to you.
Luke 6:31 (NIV)

Larue The Turtle

The Praise Pond looked so peaceful,
covered in a blanket of fog.
Larue the turtle was tucked in her shell,
asleep on a moss-covered log.

She usually spent most of her days basking in the warmth of the sun.
Watching the otters frolic and play, they seemed to have so much fun.
Larue wanted to ask if she could play, but thoughts flooded her mind.
She wasn't very sure of herself.
Maybe it was best to just stay behind.
Larue the turtle was loving and kind, but no one had ever known.
Most of the time she would hide in her shell,
but she was tired of being alone.

Larue plopped into the cool water and talked to God in prayer.
She knew that He could hear her.
She could feel His love in the air.

Larue had always been different. A little quirky, you might say.
But God showed her we're all unique,
and she learned to love herself that day.
With her newfound confidence, she felt special instead of odd.
She was so very thankful for her relationship with God.
The otters splashed in the water, getting ready for a race.
Larue swam over to play with them. A huge smile was on her face.

Because Larue was a turtle and they knew she would be slow,
They placed her on one otter's back and yelled, "READY, SET, GO!"
Racing across the Praise Pond, the mist was blowing onto her shell.
Because of God, her world had changed, and Larue couldn't wait to tell.

I will praise you,
For I am fearfully and wonderfully made.
Psalm 139:14 (NKJ)

T.J. The Bullfrog

The sun was bright. The air was hot. The water refreshing and cool.
T.J. climbed up on a lily pad and pondered what to do.
He wanted to play with the other bullfrogs and leap from pad to pad.
But sometimes he lagged a little behind,
and that made him feel a bit sad.

T.J. was sick as a baby tadpole, and his legs didn't grow quite as strong.
He tried so hard to keep up with his friends.
He wanted to feel he belonged.

Down by the Praise Pond he talked to God in the stillness of the day.
He shared with God what was on his heart as he began to pray.
"Dear God, why am I different? Why did this happen to me?
I want to be like the other bullfrogs, catching flies and being carefree.
I can't jump as far as they do, and when I try my legs don't work right.
It's all I can do just to keep up, and sometimes I cry at night."

Then, T.J. felt something special, like a whisper on the wind.
He knew that Jesus was with him and that He was his very best friend.
God says all things are created by Him and all He created was good.
After spending time with God, T.J. finally understood.
He learned that our strength comes from God.
It doesn't depend on our size.
That's when T.J. lifted up his head and looked at his life with new eyes.
God makes each of us special. We all have a job to do.
To tell the world about Jesus and that the words of the Bible are true.

Now, T.J. plays at the Praise Pond, jumping lily pads and catching flies. When we put our trust in Jesus, He can do great things with our lives.

I can do all things through Christ who strengthens me.
Phillipians 4:13 (NKJV)

Sunday At The Praise Pond

Phoebe the firefly stirred when the sun began to shine.
The bluebirds sang a melody from high up in the pine.
Phoebe spread her tiny wings as the breeze began to blow.
Excited by what the day would bring, she was ready to go.
The sky was blue. The clouds were white.
The air was warm and sweet.
She saw the pond just up ahead. Her time with God was a treat.
Phoebe floated above the pond with its lily pads of green.
Dancing sunlight on the water was such a pretty scene.
The Praise Pond was so full of life with creatures all around.
They sang their praises to the Lord. Oh, what a joyful sound!

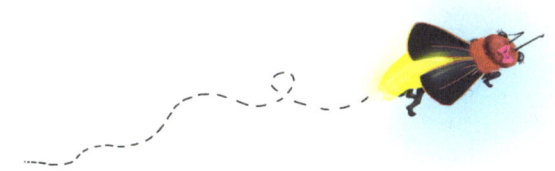

It was Sunday at the Praise Pond and excitement filled the air.
All the critters began to gather, with blessings from God to share.
You could hear the buzz of honeybees as they swirled around the hive.
And Webster was over by the bank, ready to take a dive.
Standing in the shallows was Ace the whooping crane.
All of his family by his side, he was happy that they came.
Across the pond was T.J. the frog, sitting with his mom and dad.
Enjoying the coolness of the shade, floating on a lily pad.
Lucybelle the butterfly was feeling happy and free.
She made her way to the pond, fluttering through the trees.
Larue the turtle was slow and steady, determined to make her way.
Nothing was going to keep Larue away from church today.
Ranger the duck circled the pond, quacking to one and all.
Greeting the critters as they arrived was definitely Ranger's call.
They could see Phoebe the firefly as she came floating in.
Her little light was blinking bright as service was about to begin.
A wise old owl named Oscar gave a hoot and lifted his wing.
"We're all here today to worship God, let's lift our voices and sing!"
The frogs were croaking, the birds were chirping,
and the bees were buzzing too.
Ducks were quacking, otters were splashing,
and the joy in their hearts grew.
Smiling and making a joyful noise, they knew that God could hear.
Down by the Praise Pond, they felt God's love
and knew He was always near.

Shout for joy to the Lord, all the earth.
Worship the Lord with gladness;
come before Him with joyful songs.
Psalm 100:1-2 (NIV)

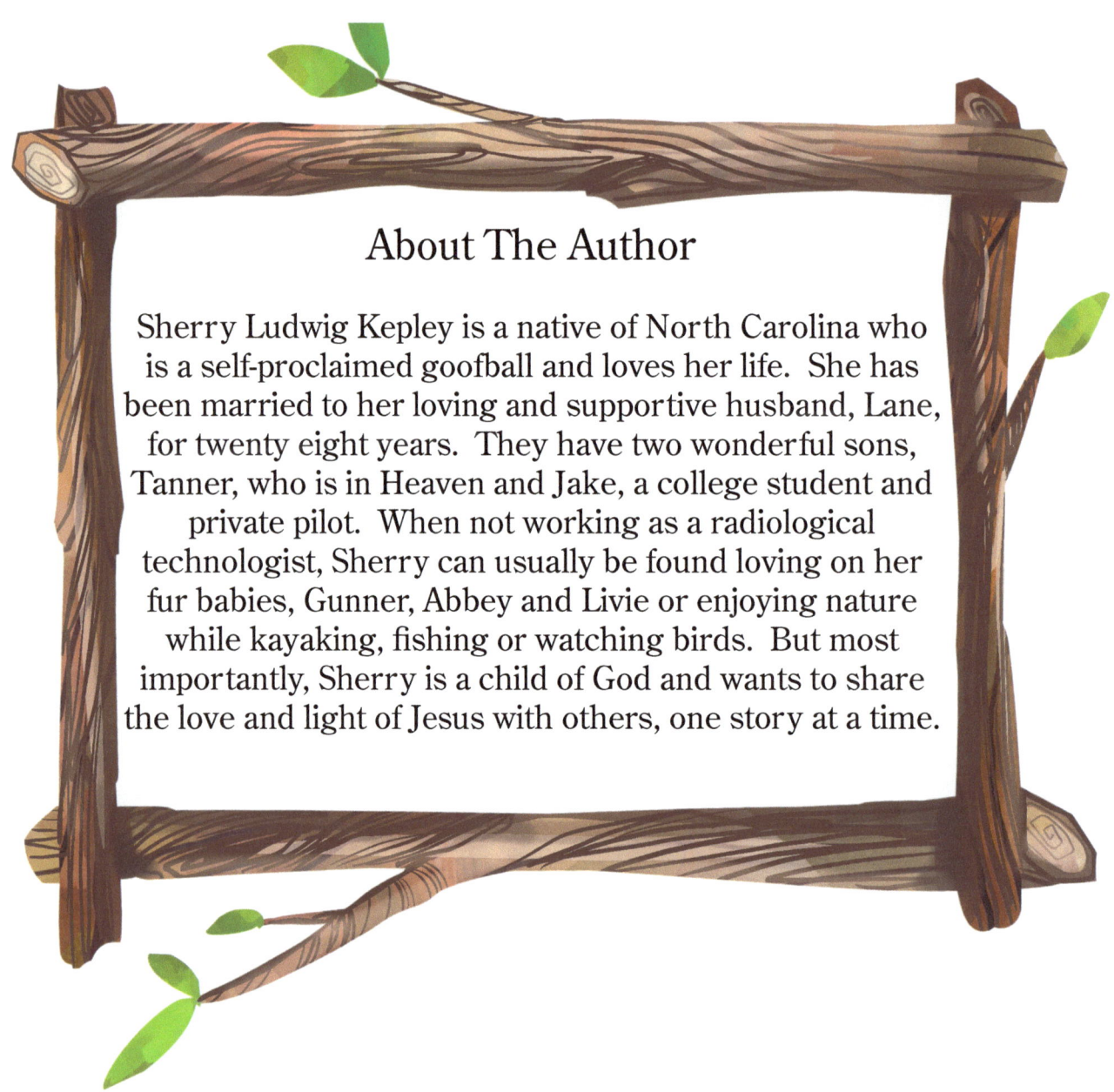

About The Author

Sherry Ludwig Kepley is a native of North Carolina who is a self-proclaimed goofball and loves her life. She has been married to her loving and supportive husband, Lane, for twenty eight years. They have two wonderful sons, Tanner, who is in Heaven and Jake, a college student and private pilot. When not working as a radiological technologist, Sherry can usually be found loving on her fur babies, Gunner, Abbey and Livie or enjoying nature while kayaking, fishing or watching birds. But most importantly, Sherry is a child of God and wants to share the love and light of Jesus with others, one story at a time.

I'd love to hear from you!

Dear Friends,
I hope you have enjoyed visiting the Praise Pond and getting to know the critters! It has been such a blessing to share them with you.
If any of the critters really spoke to you, I'd love to hear how.

You can contact me at **praisepond@outlook.com** or at this mailing address:

**Praise Pond
PO Box 179
Granite Quarry, NC 28072**

Sharing my love for Jesus is my favorite thing to do. I am available for readings and speaking as well. If you would like to read more of my writings, you can follow me on my Facebook page, **https://www.facebook.com/Tippys-Thoughts-Sharing-My-Love-For-Jesus-101032141715474**

You can also visit my website at **https://kepleylsj.wixsite.com/mysite**.

With Love from the Praise Pond,

Sherry

CPSIA information can be obtained
at www.ICGtesting.com
Printed in the USA
BVHW090224240721
612583BV00002B/4